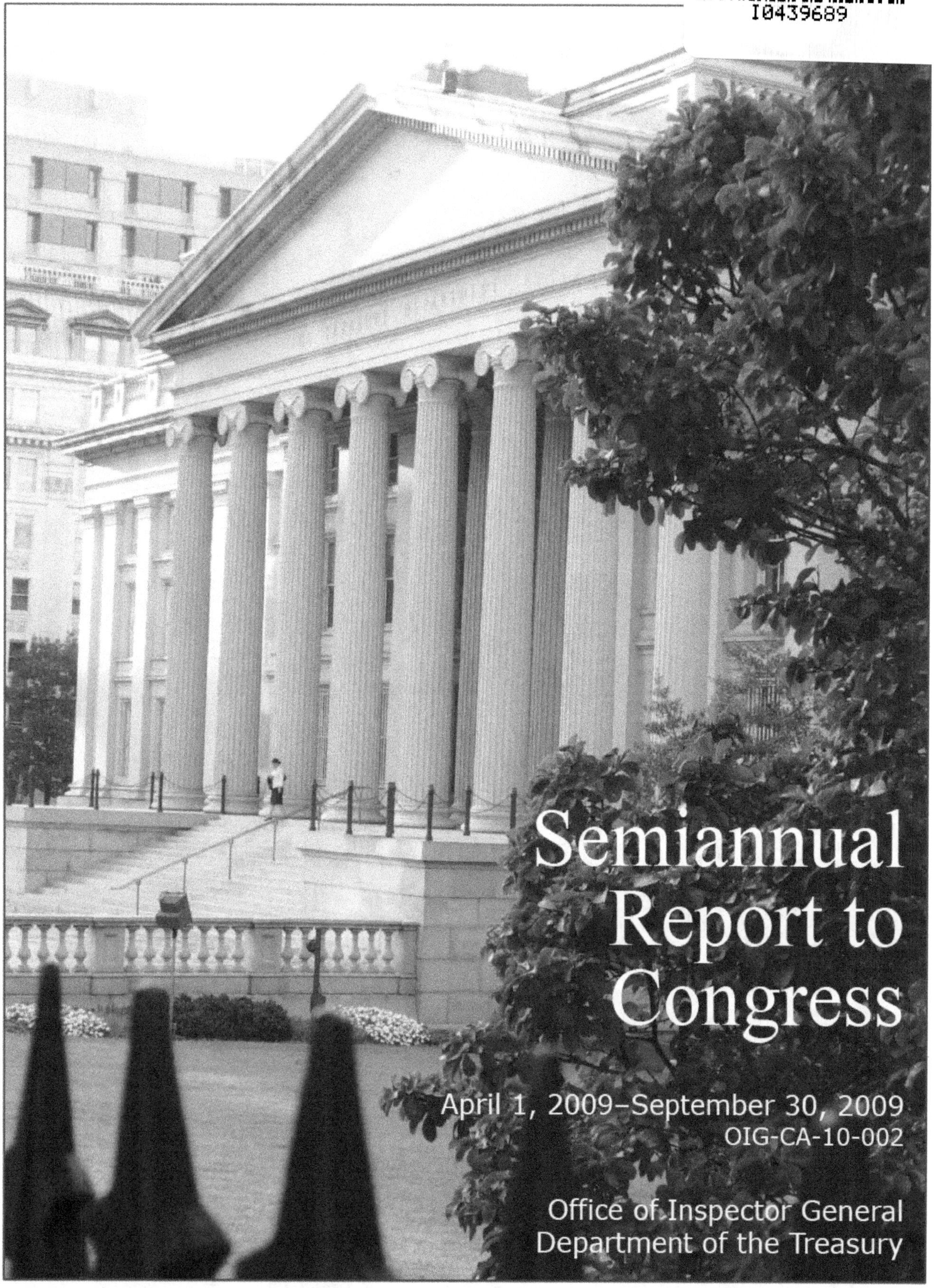

I0439689

Semiannual Report to Congress

April 1, 2009–September 30, 2009
OIG-CA-10-002

Office of Inspector General
Department of the Treasury

Highlights

During this semiannual reporting period, the Office of Audit issued 19 products, which included questioned costs of nearly $1 million, and work by the Office of Investigations resulted in two arrests; approximately $235,000 in court-ordered fines, restitution, and recoveries; and 27 personnel or administrative actions. Some of our significant results for the period are described below.

- We completed material loss reviews of six failed financial institutions that together resulted in a loss to the federal deposit insurance fund of approximately $2.48 billion. High concentrations in certain types of loans (including high-risk single-family residential loans and construction and land loans), exacerbated by significant drops in real estate values, were a key cause of five of the institutions' failures. In the other case, the institution's failure resulted from significant losses in its portfolio of preferred stock holdings in Fannie Mae and Freddie Mac. We found that the Office of Thrift Supervision and the Office of the Comptroller of the Currency (OCC) identified operational problems but were slow to take enforcement action to correct the problems.

- We issued a report on the challenges that Treasury's Office of the Fiscal Assistant Secretary has experienced in implementing a new grant in lieu of tax credit program authorized under the American Recovery and Reinvestment Act. The program calls for Treasury to distribute an estimated $16.5 billion in energy grants for certain specified energy property. Although the American Recovery and Reinvestment Act was intended to jumpstart the economy, we found—more than 5 months after the act was signed into law—that while Treasury had made progress, a fully operational program had yet to be established.

- On May 5, 2009, Inspector General Thorson and the inspectors general for the Federal Deposit Insurance Corporation and Federal Reserve System testified before the Subcommittee on Oversight and Investigations of the House Committee on Financial Services on the current threshold for material loss reviews of failed banks. In January 2009, the inspectors general sent a letter to the committee suggesting that the current threshold of $25 million, established in 1991, be raised to between $300 million and $500 million, which would free up resources for other work. Congress is considering legislation, H.R. 3330, that would, among other things, raise the threshold loss for material loss reviews to $200 million. As of September 30, 2009, H.R. 3330 had passed the House and been referred to the Senate Committee on Banking, Housing, and Urban Affairs.

- On June 12, 2009, a former OCC employee pled guilty to federal theft violations stemming from his scheme to defraud OCC by exploiting a weakness in its travel management system. The former employee was sentenced to 60 days of house arrest, 36 months of supervised probation, and 25 hours of community service and was ordered to pay $25,311 in restitution to OCC.

Message From the Inspector General

Over the past 6 months, the Department of the Treasury has continued to play a key role in the federal government's efforts to maintain the stability of the financial markets and stimulate an economic recovery. Through the Housing and Economic Recovery Act, Treasury made significant investments in mortgage giants Fannie Mae and Freddie Mac. Through the Emergency Economic Stabilization Act, more commonly known as the Troubled Assets Relief Program (TARP), Treasury has made significant investments in hundreds of financial institutions as well as in General Motors, Chrysler, and AIG. The Department has established several other programs to carry out its TARP authorities, including the Public-Private Investment Program and the Home Affordable Modification Program.

With passage of the American Recovery and Reinvestment Act, Treasury became responsible for administering an estimated $150 billion in Recovery Act direct relief, including an estimated $20 billion for low-income housing and renewable energy property grants in lieu of tax credit programs. Suffice it to say that Treasury has taken on significant new challenges and new responsibilities that have had and will continue to have an enormous impact on our economy.

The Recovery Act also established the Recovery Act Accountability and Transparency Board. The Board comprises 12 inspectors general, of which I am one. It is responsible for maintaining Recovery.gov as well as coordinating oversight of the $787 billion in Recovery Act funding. We, along with the Treasury Inspector General for Tax Administration, are committed to providing effective oversight of Treasury's Recovery Act programs. Toward that end, our office has already issued one report that identified weaknesses in Treasury's efforts to implement the renewable energy property grant in lieu of tax credit program. We also have a number of Recovery Act audits in progress. While we have noted problems, I do want to recognize the strong commitment by Deputy Secretary Wolin and Senior Accountable Officer Tangherlini to implementing effective controls over Recovery Act funds.

Just as this has been a challenging time for the Department, it has been a challenging time for my office. In addition to our Recovery Act oversight work, by law my office must perform a material loss review (MLR) within 6 months of any Treasury-regulated financial institution failure that causes a material loss ($25 million or more) to the Federal Deposit Insurance Corporation's deposit insurance fund. The purpose of an MLR is to determine why the financial institution failed and to assess the regulator's supervision.

Since September 2007, 39 Treasury-regulated institutions have failed, with estimated losses to the deposit insurance fund exceeding $27 billion. Predictions are that many more financial institutions will fail over the next couple of years. During fiscal year 2009, we completed an unprecedented 10 MLRs and, as of this writing, have another 19 in progress. This level of MLR work threatened to overwhelm our available resources. Fortunately, Congress appropriated additional resources in our fiscal year 2009 budget to enable us to hire more staff. We have been very successful in hiring many highly qualified new employees in a very short time.

Our MLR work has consistently identified irresponsible lending and unmanaged risk-taking by the financial institutions and weaknesses in supervision by their regulators. I do want to note that both Treasury regulators, the Office of the Comptroller of the Currency and the Office of Thrift Supervision, have been very responsive to the findings and recommendations from our MLRs. As the administration and Congress work toward regulatory reform, our MLR results and those of other offices of inspector general for financial regulators should be considered in determining how depository institutions should be regulated going forward.

In closing, I would like to recognize the hard work and dedication of my staff in meeting the challenges that have been presented. Especially noteworthy is the fact that we have not missed our MLR mandate even one time since the financial crisis began. Our work continues to be of the highest caliber, and our results have had and will continue to have a significant impact in helping the Department strengthen its programs and operations. I look forward to continuing to work with Secretary Geithner and Deputy Secretary Wolin in meeting the demands and challenges that remain ahead of us.

Eric M. Thorson
Inspector General

Contents

Overview of the Office of Inspector General

The Department of the Treasury's Office of Inspector General (OIG) was established pursuant to the 1988 amendment to the Inspector General Act of 1978.[1] OIG is headed by an Inspector General appointed by the President of the United States, with the advice and consent of the Senate. Serving with the Inspector General in the immediate office is a Deputy Inspector General. OIG performs independent, objective reviews of Treasury programs and operations, except for those of the Internal Revenue Service (IRS) and the Troubled Assets Relief Program (TARP), and keeps the Secretary of the Treasury and Congress fully informed of problems, deficiencies, and the need for corrective action. The Treasury Inspector General for Tax Administration performs oversight related to IRS. A special inspector general and the Government Accountability Office (GAO) perform oversight related to TARP.

OIG is organized into four divisions: (1) Office of Audit, (2) Office of Investigations, (3) Office of Counsel, and (4) Office of Management. OIG is headquartered in Washington, DC, and has an audit office in Boston, Massachusetts.

The Office of Audit performs and supervises audits, attestation engagements, and evaluations. The Assistant Inspector General for Audit has two deputies. One is primarily responsible for performance audits, and the other is primarily responsible for financial management, information technology, and financial assistance audits.

The Office of Investigations performs investigations and conducts initiatives to detect and prevent fraud, waste, and abuse in Treasury programs and operations. The Assistant Inspector General for Investigations is responsible for all investigations relating to Treasury programs and operations and integrity oversight reviews of select Treasury bureaus.

The Office of Counsel (1) processes all Freedom of Information Act/Privacy Act requests and administrative appeals on behalf of OIG; (2) processes all discovery requests for information held by OIG; (3) represents OIG in administrative Equal Employment Opportunity and Merit Systems Protection Board proceedings; (4) conducts ethics training and provides ethics advice to OIG employees and ensures OIG compliance with financial disclosure requirements; (5) reviews proposed legislation and regulations relating to the Department; (6) reviews and issues administrative subpoenas; (7) reviews and responds to all *Giglio* requests for information about Treasury personnel who may testify in trials; and (8) provides legal advice to the other OIG divisions.

The Office of Management provides services to maintain the OIG administrative infrastructure. It also manages the Treasury OIG Hotline to facilitate reporting of allegations involving Treasury programs and activities. The Assistant Inspector General for Management oversees these functions.

As of September 30, 2009, OIG had 117 full-time staff. OIG's fiscal year 2009 appropriation was $26.125 million.

---

[1] 5 U.S.C. app. 3.

Treasury Management and Performance Challenges

In accordance with the Reports Consolidation Act of 2000, the Treasury Inspector General annually provides the Secretary of the Treasury with his perspective on the most serious management and performance challenges facing the Department. The Secretary includes these challenges in Treasury's annual agency financial report. In a memorandum to Secretary Geithner dated October 29, 2009, Inspector General Thorson reported one new challenge—management of American Recovery and Reinvestment Act (Recovery Act) programs—and four challenges from last year. Two previously reported challenges were removed. The following is an abridged description of the challenges reported and removed.

Management of Treasury's New Authorities Related to Distressed Financial Markets (Repeat Challenge)

Treasury, along with the Federal Reserve, the Federal Deposit Insurance Corporation (FDIC), and the Federal Housing Finance Agency, has taken unprecedented actions to address the current financial crisis. To assist in those efforts, Congress passed the Housing and Economic Recovery Act in July 2008, which gave Treasury broad new authorities to address the distressed financial condition of Fannie Mae and Freddie Mac. Less than 6 weeks later, the Federal Housing Finance Agency put both entities into conservatorship. According to Treasury data, as of June 30, 2009, Treasury had purchased $86.5 billion in preferred stock of the two entities to cover their continuing losses and maintain a positive net worth. Treasury also purchased $154.2 billion of mortgage-backed

securities issued by Fannie Mae and Freddie Mac. Even with this assistance, both entities remain in a weakened financial condition and may require more assistance.

As the turmoil in the financial markets increased, Treasury and the Federal Reserve took additional actions to deal with the situation, including rescuing Bear Stearns and AIG. Treasury also sought and obtained additional authorities through passage of the Emergency Economic Stabilization Act (EESA) in October 2008. EESA, commonly known as TARP, gave the Treasury Secretary $700 billion to, among other things, (1) purchase capital in qualifying U.S.-controlled financial institutions and (2) buy, maintain, and sell toxic mortgage-related assets from financial institutions.

After EESA was enacted, the Department aggressively moved forward to loosen the credit market by purchasing senior preferred stock in nine of the nation's largest financial institutions. Since then, hundreds of other financial institutions have also participated in the Capital Purchase Program (CPP). To date, some CPP participants have repurchased preferred shares and warrants totaling more than $70 billion. However, a small but growing number of CPP recipients are failing to make their 5 percent dividend payments due to Treasury.

EESA established a special inspector general for TARP and imposed oversight and periodic reporting requirements on both the special inspector general and GAO. Under EESA, GAO is also responsible for performing the annual financial statement audit of TARP. Recently, GAO reported that at the 1-year mark, TARP in general and CPP in particular, along with other efforts by the Federal Reserve and FDIC, had made important contributions to help stabilize credit markets. However, GAO also reported that many challenges and uncertainties remain. GAO further noted that other programs, such as the Public-Private Investment Program and the Home Affordable Modification Program, still face implementation or operational challenges. GAO recommended that as Treasury considers further action under TARP, including whether to extend the program beyond December 31, 2009, the Department should evaluate the program in the broader context of efforts by the Federal Reserve and FDIC to stabilize the financial system.

The Department is working through several significant accounting issues involving some very complex TARP transactions. As a result, the Department, in consultation with our office and GAO, has requested an extension from the Office of Management and Budget (OMB) for its fiscal year 2009 annual financial reporting submission.

As conditions improve, Treasury will need to work with its partners to disassemble the structure established to support recovery efforts and ensure that federal funds no longer needed for those efforts are returned in an orderly manner to the Treasury general fund.

Regulation of National Banks and Thrifts (Repeat Challenge)

Since September 2007, 39 Treasury-regulated financial institutions have failed, with estimated losses to the deposit insurance fund exceeding $27 billion. Even more financial institutions are expected to fail over the next 2 years.

Although many factors have contributed to the turmoil in the financial markets, Treasury's

Office of the Comptroller of the Currency (OCC) and Office of Thrift Supervision (OTS) did not identify early or force timely correction of unsafe and unsound practices by institutions under their supervision. The irresponsible lending practices of many institutions are now well-recognized—including reliance on risky products, such as option adjustable rate mortgages, and degradation of underwriting standards. At the same time, financial institutions engaged in other high-risk activities, including high asset concentrations in commercial real estate and overreliance on unpredictable brokered deposits to fund rapid growth. There have also been instances of certain ailing thrifts backdating capital contributions.

The banking industry will continue to be stressed over the next several years. The next substantial stresses to financial markets may result from troubled credit card debt and further deterioration in commercial real estate loans and could significantly affect financial institutions that had limited exposure to the housing crisis.

Our office is mandated to review failures of Treasury-regulated financial institutions that result in material losses to the deposit insurance fund. As of October 29, 2009, we have completed 12 such reviews and are engaged in 19 others. These reviews identify the causes of the failures and assess supervision exercised over failed institutions. Both OCC and OTS have been responsive to our recommendations for improving supervision. For example, OTS has issued guidance addressing concentration issues and the appropriate accounting treatment for capital contributions. However, these reviews do not address the broader supervisory effectiveness of the federal banking regulators as a whole or the effectiveness of the supervisory structure. It is therefore essential that OCC and OTS continue to take a critical look at their supervisory processes to identify why those processes did not prevent or mitigate the practices that led to the current crisis and what can be done to better protect the financial health of the banking industry and consumers going forward.

Recognizing that the focus of EESA and the Recovery Act is on the current crisis, another consideration is the need to identify, monitor, and manage emerging domestic and global systemic economic risks. Moreover, these emerging risks may go beyond the current U.S. regulatory structure. Treasury and its regulatory partners must continue to diligently monitor both regulated and unregulated products and markets for new systemic risks that may require action.

Finally, both the administration and Congress are considering proposals for regulatory reform, ranging from the creation of a single financial regulator to a more limited approach calling for oversight councils composed of the existing regulators and consolidating OTS and OCC. Also under consideration is transferring responsibility for consumer financial protection functions to a new regulatory agency. Treasury, OCC, and OTS will need to work in concert with the other affected federal bank regulators to ensure a smooth and effective transition to the new regulatory structure that emerges.

Management of Recovery Act Programs (New Challenge)

Treasury is responsible for overseeing an estimated $150 billion of Recovery Act funding and tax relief. Treasury's oversight responsibilities include grants for specified

energy property in lieu of tax credits, grants to states for low-income housing projects in lieu of tax credits, increased Community Development Financial Institutions Fund grants and tax credits, economic recovery payments to social security beneficiaries and others, and payments to U.S. territories for distribution to their citizens. Many of these programs are new to Treasury and involve very large dollar amounts. As a result, Treasury faces immense challenges in ensuring that the programs achieve their intended purposes, provide for accountability and transparency, and are free from fraud and abuse.

Treasury's Recovery Act grants in lieu of tax credit programs—for specified energy property and to states for low-income housing projects—are estimated to cost almost $20 billion over their lives. Treasury has dedicated only a small number of staff to award and monitor these funds. We have concerns that the current staffing level is not commensurate with the size of these programs.

The Deputy Secretary and the Senior Accountability Officer have shown a strong commitment to implementing an effective control structure over Recovery Act activities and strong support for our oversight effort.

Management of Capital Investments (Repeat Challenge)

Managing large capital investments, particularly information technology investments, is a difficult challenge for any organization, whether public or private. In prior years, we have reported on a number of capital investment projects that either failed or had serious problems. Treasury is now making the transition to a new, mission-critical telecommunications system, TNet. The overall value of the TNet contract is estimated at $270 million. The transition, however, is now nearly 2 years late. Treasury must exercise continuous vigilance in managing its capital investments.

Anti-Money Laundering and Terrorist Financing/Bank Secrecy Act Enforcement (Repeat Challenge)

Treasury faces unique challenges in carrying out its responsibilities under the Bank Secrecy Act (BSA) and USA Patriot Act to prevent and detect money laundering and terrorist financing. Although the Financial Crimes Enforcement Network (FinCEN) is responsible for administering BSA, a large number of other federal and state entities participate in efforts to ensure compliance with BSA. Many of these entities also participate in efforts to ensure compliance with U.S. foreign sanction programs administered by Treasury's Office of Foreign Assets Control (OFAC).

FinCEN and OFAC have entered into memoranda of understanding with many federal and state regulators in an attempt to build a consistent and effective process. However, these instruments are nonbinding and carry no penalties for violations.

Although BSA reports are critical to law enforcement, past audits have shown that many contain incomplete or erroneous data and that examination coverage by financial institution regulators of BSA compliance has been limited.

Given the criticality of this management challenge to the Department's mission, we continue to consider BSA and OFAC programs as inherently high-risk. Adding to this risk in the current environment is the risk that financial institutions and their regulators may decrease their attention to BSA and OFAC program compliance as they address safety and soundness concerns. As the administration and Congress consider what could be sweeping changes to the financial regulatory structure, those changes must ensure that BSA and OFAC compliance examination coverage is sufficient.

Challenges Removed

We removed corporate management as an overarching management challenge, first identified as a challenge in 2004, because the Department has made significant progress in building up a sustainable corporate control structure. We also removed information security as a management and performance challenge, first identified in 2001, because Treasury has made significant strides in improving and institutionalizing its information security controls.

Significant Audits and Evaluations

Financial Management

Financial Audits

The Chief Financial Officers Act, as amended by the Government Management Reform Act, requires annual financial statement audits of Treasury and OMB–designated entities. In this regard, OMB has designated IRS for annual financial statement audits. The financial statements of certain other Treasury component entities are audited pursuant to other requirements or due to their materiality to Treasury's consolidated financial statements or other reasons. The following table shows audit results for fiscal years 2008 and 2007.

Treasury-audited financial statements and related audits						
	Fiscal year 2008 audit results			Fiscal year 2007 audit results		
Entity	Opinion	Material weaknesses	Other significant deficiencies	Opinion	Material weaknesses	Other significant deficiencies
Government Management Reform Act/Chief Financial Officers Act requirements						
Department of the Treasury	UQ	1	2	UQ	1	2
Internal Revenue Service (A)	UQ	3	1	UQ	4	1
Other required audits						
Bureau of Engraving and Printing	UQ	0	0	UQ	0	0
Community Development Financial Institutions Fund (B)	UQ	0	2	D	0	2
Office of DC Pensions	UQ	0	0	UQ	0	0
Exchange Stabilization Fund	UQ	1	1	UQ	0	0
Federal Financing Bank	UQ	0	0	UQ	0	0
Office of the Comptroller of the Currency	UQ	0	0	UQ	0	1
Office of Thrift Supervision	UQ	0	0	UQ	0	0
Treasury Forfeiture Fund	UQ	0	0	UQ	0	2
Mint						
Financial statements	UQ	0	2	UQ	1	0
Custodial gold and silver reserves	UQ	0	0	UQ	0	0
Other audited accounts that are material to Treasury financial statements						
Bureau of the Public Debt						
Schedule of Federal Debt (A)	UQ	0	0	UQ	0	0
Government trust funds	UQ	0	1	UQ	0	0
Financial Management Service						
Treasury-managed accounts	UQ	0	1	UQ	0	0
Operating cash of the federal government	UQ	0	0	UQ	0	1
Management-initiated audit						
FinCEN	UQ	0	0	UQ	1	0
UQ	Unqualified opinion					
D	Disclaimer of opinion					
(A)	Audited by GAO					
(B)	Audit of the Statement of Financial Position only for fiscal year 2008, full-scope audit of all financial statements for fiscal year 2007					

Audits of the fiscal year 2009 financial statements or schedules of the Department and component reporting entities were in progress at the end of this semiannual reporting period.

The following instances of noncompliance with the Federal Financial Management Improvement Act, which all relate to IRS, were reported in connection with the audit of the Department's fiscal year 2008 consolidated financial statements. The status of these noncompliances, including progress in implementing remediation plans, will be evaluated as part of the audit of Treasury's fiscal year 2009 financial statements.

Condition	Type of noncompliance
Financial management systems do not provide timely and reliable information for financial reporting and preparation of financial statements. IRS had to rely on extensive compensating procedures to generate reliable financial statements. (first reported in fiscal year 1997)	Federal financial management systems requirements
Deficiencies were identified in information security controls, resulting in increased risk of unauthorized individuals accessing, altering, or abusing proprietary IRS programs and electronic data and taxpayer information. (first reported in fiscal year 1997)	Federal financial management systems requirements
Material weaknesses related to controls over unpaid tax assessments exist. (first reported in fiscal year 1997)	Federal accounting standards
Financial management system cannot produce reliable, current information on the costs of IRS activities to support decision making on a routine basis, consistent with the requirements of Statement of Federal Financial Accounting Standards No. 4, Managerial Cost Accounting Standards. (first reported in fiscal year 1998)	Federal accounting standards
IRS's core general ledger system for tax-related activities does not comply with the U.S. Government Standard General Ledger at the transaction level and also does not post transactions in conformance with Standard General Ledger posting models. (first reported in fiscal year 1997)	U.S. Government Standard General Ledger

Reports on the Processing of Transactions by BPD

Three reports described below were completed in support of the audit of Treasury's fiscal year 2009 consolidated financial statements and the financial statement audits of certain other federal agencies.

An independent public accountant (IPA) under our supervision examined the accounting processing and general computer controls related to financial management services provided to various federal agencies by the Bureau of the Public Debt's (BPD) Administrative Resource Center. The IPA found that (1) the description of controls for these activities fairly presented, in all material respects, the controls that had been placed in operation as of June 30, 2009; (2) the controls were suitably designed; and (3) the controls tested by the IPA were effective from July 1, 2008, to June 30, 2009. The IPA noted no instances of reportable noncompliance with laws and regulations tested. **(OIG-09-045)**

An IPA under our supervision performed examinations that covered the general computer and investment/redemption processing controls related to BPD's transactions processing of investment accounts for various federal agencies and the general computer and trust fund management processing controls related to BPD's transactions processing of investment accounts of various federal and state agencies. The IPA found that (1) BPD's description of these controls fairly presented, in all material respects, the controls that had been placed in operation as of July 31, 2009; (2) the controls were suitably designed; and (3) the controls tested by the IPA were effective during the period August 1, 2008, to July 31, 2009. The IPA noted no instances of reportable noncompliance with the laws and regulations tested. **(OIG-09-049, OIG-09-050)**

Information Technology

Fiscal Year 2009 Evaluations of Treasury's FISMA Implementation for Its Intelligence Program and Non-IRS Collateral National Security Systems

We completed two Federal Information Security Management Act (FISMA) independent evaluations during this reporting period covering the Department's intelligence program and non-IRS collateral national security systems. We found that Treasury addressed a majority of findings cited in our prior-year reports. However, we identified 6 areas in the intelligence program and 8 areas with the collateral systems where the information security programs and practices need to be improved. Treasury management concurred with our recommendations to address these matters. Both reports are designated Sensitive But Unclassified. **(OIG-09-051, OIG-CA-09-011)**

FMS's Database Management Systems Have Weaknesses in Key Controls

We determined that Financial Management Service's(FMS) database management systems had weaknesses in key security controls over its database management systems. Specifically, database patches were not applied in a timely manner, database users were granted excessive privileges, account and password management

was not effective, and security controls over a legacy system were inadequate. FMS concurred with our recommendations to address these matters. **(OIG-CA-09-012)**

Programs and Operations

Bank Failures and Material Loss Reviews

OCC and OTS share responsibility with the FDIC and the Federal Reserve for regulating and supervising banks and thrifts in the United States. OCC regulates national chartered banks and OTS regulates thrifts, while FDIC and the Federal Reserve share regulation of state-chartered banks and thrifts. State regulatory authorities may also share responsibility for regulating and supervising banks and thrifts.

In 1991, Congress enacted the Federal Deposit Insurance Corporation Improvement Act (FDICIA) amending the Federal Deposit Insurance Act following the failures of about 1,000 banks and thrifts between 1986 and 1990 that resulted in billions of dollars in losses to the deposit insurance fund. The amendments require that banking regulators take specified supervisory actions when they identify unsafe or unsound practices or conditions.

Section 38(k) of FDICIA requires that the inspectors general of Treasury, FDIC, and the Federal Reserve review the failures of depository institutions when the estimated loss to the deposit insurance fund becomes material (defined as a loss that exceeds the greater of $25 million or 2 percent of the institution's total assets). As part of the material loss review (MLR), we determine the causes of the failure and assess the supervision over the institution, including the implementation of the Prompt Corrective Action (PCA) provisions in

FDICIA;[2] and make recommendations for preventing any such loss in the future. The MLR must be completed within 6 months.

Since 2007, FDIC and other regulators have closed 133 banks and thrifts. Thirty-nine (39) of these institutions were regulated by Treasury. In prior semiannual reports, we reported on 5 MLRs completed during the current crisis. During the current semi-annual reporting period, we completed 6 MLRs, 4 supervised by OTS and 2 supervised by OCC, which are described in more detail below. As of September 30, 2009, we had 18 ongoing MLRs, and we expect additional bank and thrift failures in the coming months.

From the 11 MLRs completed as of September 30, 2009, we have seen several trends emerge. With respect to the causes of institutions' failures, we found overly aggressive growth strategies; risky lending products, such as option adjustable rate mortgages, coupled with inadequate risk management and unsound underwriting; high concentrations in areas such as commercial real estate; and heavy reliance on more costly wholesale funding, such as Federal Home Loan Bank loans and brokered deposits. In one instance, we found that a national bank failed because of the losses incurred with its preferred stock holdings in Fannie Mae and Freddie Mac. With respect to supervision, we found that regulators conducted regular and

---

[2] PCA is a framework of supervisory actions, set forth in 12 U.S.C. § 1831, for insured depository institutions that are not adequately capitalized. It was intended to ensure that action is taken when an institution becomes financially troubled in order to prevent a failure or minimize resulting losses. These actions become increasingly severe as the institution falls into lower capital categories. The capital categories are well-capitalized, adequately capitalized, undercapitalized, significantly undercapitalized, and critically undercapitalized.

timely examinations and identified operational problems, but were slow to take enforcement actions to correct the problems. We also noted that regulators took the appropriate PCA actions when warranted but those actions did not save the institutions. While it is too soon to comment on the effectiveness of the PCA provisions of FDICIA more generally, this is an area we believe should be examined further.

OTS-Regulated Institutions Reviewed

Downey Savings and Loan Association, FA, of Newport Beach, California (closed November 21, 2008; estimated loss to the deposit insurance fund - $1.4 billion)

The primary causes of Downey's failure were the thrift's high concentrations in single-family residential loans, which included concentrations in option adjustable rate mortgage loans, reduced documentation loans, subprime loans, and loans with layered risk; inadequate risk-monitoring systems; the thrift's unresponsiveness to OTS recommendations; and high turnover in the thrift's management. The drop in real estate values in Downey's markets exacerbated these conditions.

OTS conducted an internal failed bank review as required by its policy. The OTS review found that a more forceful regulatory response is warranted when thrifts have concentrations of higher-risk nontraditional mortgage products. We affirm OTS's internal findings and the need for corrective action, particularly the need for more definitive guidance on concentration risk for nontraditional mortgage loans and OTS's authority to address thrifts taking excessive risks in these loan products.

In addition, we found that OTS did not follow its existing guidance for taking enforcement action when it issued an informal rather than formal enforcement action in 2006. OTS examiners told us that they exercised their regulatory discretion in taking informal rather than formal enforcement action. OTS examiners also told us that the institution became more responsive to OTS's supervision and that OTS accomplished the same results as if formal enforcement action had been taken. We agreed that the informal action taken was strong; however, OTS did not follow its own written guidance to the letter.

We concluded that OTS appropriately used its authority under PCA when it issued a cease and desist order in September 2008. The order, among other things, reclassified Downey's capital level to adequately capitalized and imposed restrictions even though the thrift's capital level at the time met the definition of well-capitalized.

We recommended that OTS ensure that the recommendations from its internal assessment of the Downey failure are implemented and that the lessons learned described in that assessment are taken into account going forward. In this regard, OTS should direct examiners to closely review and monitor thrifts that refuse to establish appropriate limits for concentrations that pose significant risk and pursue corrective action when concentration limits are not reasonable. Additionally, OTS should assess the need for more guidance for examiners on determining materiality of concentrations and determining appropriate examiner response to high-risk concentrations, including when to impose absolute limits to prevent excessive concentration. OTS should formally communicate to the industry the guidance in New Directions Bulletin 06-14, Concentrations of Risks, as to OTS's expectation that concentration measurements and limits be set as

a percentage of capital, not just as a percentage of total assets or loans. OTS should also communicate the need for a sound internal risk management system for higher-risk concentrations.

OTS concurred with and has implemented our recommendation by issuing further guidance regarding concentrations to the thrift industry and to OTS staff that addresses asset and liability concentration issues described in our report and identified internally by OTS. **(OIG-09-039)**

PFF Bank and Trust of Pomona, California (closed November 21, 2008; estimated loss to the deposit insurance fund - $729.6 million)

The primary causes of PFF's failure were its high concentration in construction and land loans and related credit losses and its inadequate capital relative to the levels of risk on its loans. The drop in real estate values in PFF's markets exacerbated these conditions.

A stronger supervisory response to PFF's concentration in construction and land loans was warranted. OTS did not take timely action on PFF's inadequate capital levels when it may have made a difference. By 2008, PFF's condition had worsened to the point that formal enforcement action was warranted under OTS guidance. However, OTS delayed taking formal enforcement action, pursuing instead various informal enforcement actions, because PFF was in the process of being acquired by an investor. Although the planned acquisition ultimately did not occur, we concluded that OTS's exercise of regulatory discretion (taking informal rather than formal enforcement action) was reasonable. We also concluded that OTS used its authority under PCA in an appropriate and timely manner.

OTS conducted an internal failed bank review, which concluded that OTS did not effectively follow up on its October 2002 limited examination regarding PFF's high concentrations. OTS's review found that its guidance should emphasize the need for a sound internal risk management system for higher-risk concentrations. We affirmed OTS's internal findings and the need for corrective action.

In addition to implementing corrective actions from its internal review, we recommended that OTS should formally communicate to the industry the guidance in New Directions Bulletin 06-14 as to OTS's expectation that concentration measurements and limits be set as a percentage of capital, not just as a percentage of total assets or loans. OTS should also communicate the need for a sound internal risk management system for higher-risk concentrations.

OTS concurred with and has implemented our recommendation by issuing further guidance regarding concentrations to the thrift industry and to OTS staff that addresses asset and liability concentration issues described in our report and identified internally by OTS. **(OIG-09-038)**

Suburban Federal Savings Bank of Crofton, Maryland (closed January 30, 2009; estimated lost to the deposit insurance fund - $126 million)

Suburban's failure was caused primarily by significant loan delinquencies and losses in speculative and high-risk acquisition, development, and construction loans. Suburban pursued an aggressive growth strategy in these loans from 2003 until 2007, when it transitioned from traditional mortgage lending into mortgage banking. During this period, Suburban's acquisition, development, and construction loan assets more than doubled. While pursuing this growth, Suburban's board and management did not establish adequate internal controls over its operations and accounting systems, resulting in failure to recognize, properly report, or correct the thrift's deteriorating financial position. As a result, when the real estate market it served took a downturn in 2007, Suburban was particularly vulnerable and the losses ultimately led to its demise.

OTS's supervision did not adequately address Suburban's problems early enough to prevent a material loss to the deposit insurance fund. OTS's examinations and oversight identified the thrift's problems, including concerns with Suburban's aggressive growth strategy in highly concentrated, speculative acquisition, development, and construction loans and weaknesses in its internal controls. However, Suburban did not sufficiently correct problems and OTS did not adequately monitor the thrift's actions through field visits to ensure that corrections were made.

OTS repeatedly recommended corrective actions through matters requiring board attention. In July 2007, OTS took informal enforcement action with a Troubled Condition and Directive letter. In March 2008, OTS took formal enforcement action through a cease and desist order. By then it was too late to prevent the thrift from failing. In 2007, OTS also considered but did not assess civil money penalties, deciding to pursue them only if the thrift did not comply with the Troubled Condition and Directive letter and the cease and desist order.

We also concluded that OTS appropriately and timely initiated PCA action when Suburban fell below the well-capitalized level in 2008 by requiring Suburban to file a capital restoration plan and abide by various restrictions. The thrift's plan determined that the only solution to its undercapitalized state was to find a merger partner. When that effort failed, OTS took timely action to appoint FDIC as receiver.

OTS conducted an internal failed bank review of Suburban in accordance with its policy. OTS's internal review found that Suburban's failure resulted primarily from ineffective management and board oversight in a period of aggressive, high-risk growth extending from 2003 to 2007. OTS's review concluded that it (1) did not take timely enforcement action, (2) failed to conduct adequate follow-up with Suburban to ensure that matters requiring board attention were resolved in a timely manner, and (3) did not effectively control asset concentration by requiring concentration limits as a percentage of capital. Our MLR affirmed OTS's internal findings and the need for earlier corrective action.

In addition to implementing corrective actions from its internal review, we recommended that OTS ensure (1) regional offices more closely monitor and scrutinize thrift financial reports and consider appropriate enforcement action, including civil money penalties, when chronic errors are found and (2) examiners conduct timely and appropriately scoped field visits to thrifts with repeat problems and elevate the supervisory response, to include enforcement action when necessary, if the field visits find that corrective action has not been taken.

OTS concurred with our recommendations and committed to take necessary action to address them. OTS issued new internal guidelines in May 2009 for Enforcement Review Committee meetings to ensure consistent implementation and resolution of enforcement actions. OTS also issued guidance through a memorandum to thrift chief executive officers in July 2009 on asset and liability concentrations and related risk management practices. **(OIG-09-047)**

Ameribank, Inc. of Northfork, West Virginia (closed September 19, 2008; estimated loss to the deposit insurance fund - $33.4 million)

The primary causes of Ameribank's failure were the thrift's rapid growth in assets and an unsafe and unsound concentration in construction rehabilitation account loans resulting from its failure to appropriately manage its relationship with a third-party mortgage broker, LendingOne. Ameribank's board and management did not exercise sufficient oversight of the LendingOne relationship. A weak internal loan review process and weak underwriting standards also contributed to the thrift's failure. The deterioration in the credit market and decline of the real estate market exacerbated these conditions.

OTS's supervision of the thrift failed to prevent a material loss to the deposit insurance fund. The thrift's high-risk business strategy should have warranted more careful and earlier attention to address its rapid growth in high-risk concentrations. OTS did not adequately sample the LendingOne loans prior to the April 2007 examination and did not thoroughly review the thrift's agreement with LendingOne until 2007, even though Ameribank's relationship with LendingOne extended back to 2003. In addition, the LendingOne construction rehabilitation account loans were not properly categorized, and OTS's guidance on those loans was not specific.

OTS also conducted an internal review which determined the main causes of Ameribank's failure as credit losses, the lack of sound risk management practices that arose primarily out of the LendingOne relationship, and the beginning of the deterioration and turmoil in the credit markets in 2007. We affirmed OTS's internal findings and need for corrective actions.

In addition to implementing corrective actions from its internal review, we recommended that OTS remind its examiners of guidance covering the risks associated with rapid growth in high-risk concentrations, the need to conduct more thorough loan sampling from the portfolio when a rapid increase in concentration is identified, and the need to assess thrift third-party relationships. We also recommended that OTS evaluate the need for guidance requiring risk assessment of construction rehabilitation account loans as an integral part of assessing a thrift's overall risk. OTS concurred with our recommendations. **(OIG-09-036)**

OCC-Regulated Institutions Reviewed

Ocala National Bank of Ocala, Florida (closed January 30, 2009; estimated loss to the deposit insurance fund - $99.6 million)

Ocala National Bank failed because of significant losses within its construction and land development loan portfolio. The bank grew rapidly from 2004 to 2006, largely due to the increased number and high concentration of these loans. The bank's management, however, did not adequately control concentration risk or ensure that credit underwriting and administrative controls were adequate. The decline in the real estate market and the secondary loan market exacerbated these deficiencies.

OCC's supervision of Ocala National Bank did not prevent a material loss to the deposit insurance fund. OCC identified problems early at the bank, but the actions taken by the bank were not sufficient. OCC identified areas needing correction, but its supervisory approach from 2005 through 2007 was primarily to rely on examiner recommendations and matters requiring attention in the reports of examination. From 2005 through 2006, OCC also continued to assign the bank a CAMELS composite rating of 2, the same rating assigned in 2004, when relatively few problems were noted.[3] This proved to be an ineffective strategy, and the bank's problems persisted and worsened until its ultimate failure in 2009.

OCC was reluctant to take more forceful action earlier because prior to 2007 the bank was profitable and asset quality problems were not yet readily apparent. While we understand the judgment involved, in retrospect we believe that a more forceful approach should have been used sooner, given the bank's circumstances.

We also identified two other matters that negatively affected Ocala National Bank but financially benefited the owner and board members. First, in 2007, while the bank was incurring a net operating loss of $2.3 million, it paid dividends of $3.9 million to the bank's holding company, some of which may have been unallowed. The owner and his family were the majority shareholders of the holding company. Second, the bank made payments

---

[3] CAMELS is an acronym for performance rating components for financial institutions: Capital adequacy, Asset quality, Management administration, Earnings, Liquidity, and Sensitivity to market risk. Numerical values range from 1 to 5, with 1 being the best rating and 5 being the worst. Each institution is also assigned a composite rating based on an assessment of its overall condition and level of supervisory concern.

totaling approximately $1 million to a company partly owned by the bank owner's son and several bank board members to repurchase the company's portion of loans, some of which were nonperforming, while the bank's financial condition was deteriorating. We believe that OCC should have more aggressively examined both of these matters. We also noted that OCC guidance does not require examiners to expand procedures to include a more detailed review of dividends or payments made to related organizations for troubled or high-risk banks.

OCC acted forcefully against the bank in early 2008, when it appropriately used its authority under PCA. Specifically, OCC's February 2008 consent order reclassified Ocala National Bank's capital level to adequately capitalized, which prohibited the bank from accepting or renewing brokered deposits without a waiver from FDIC. (In the case of Ocala National Bank, FDIC did grant a waiver in May 2008 to last until August 2008.)

We recommended that OCC (1) caution examiners and supervisors that decisions to assign the same CAMELS component and composite ratings as in prior examinations and refrain from taking enforcement action when conditions at a bank have deteriorated need to be well-justified and documented in the examination workpapers and (2) remind examiners that it is prudent to expand examination procedures for troubled or high-risk banks to review the appropriateness of (a) dividends and (b) payments to related organizations, particularly when the dividends or payments may benefit bank management and board members. In this regard, OCC should reassess its examination guidance concerning review of dividends and related organizations.

OCC agreed that there were shortcomings in its supervision and that it is appropriate to reinforce certain principles to its examining staff. OCC stated that senior management used a national examiner conference call to illustrate for examiners, through the experience of earlier bank failures, the importance of being assertive in identifying and following through on identified weaknesses in a timely manner. OCC indicated that it would continue this message through examiner briefings, future examiner conference calls, and as other opportunities arise. OCC also stated that heightened scrutiny of certain dividends and payments to related organizations is appropriate. OCC said that it would reinforce this message to examiners during one of its regular national conference calls. **(OIG-09-043)**

National Bank of Commerce of Berkeley, Illinois (closed January 16, 2009; estimated loss to the deposit insurance fund - $92.5 million)

The primary cause of National Bank of Commerce's (NBC) failure was its significant losses from preferred stock holdings in Fannie Mae and Freddie Mac. These losses depleted the bank's capital and strained its liquidity. In the end, after several attempts, NBC was unable to raise capital or obtain financial assistance to prevent its closure.

We found that the scope of OCC's examinations of NBC appeared comprehensive as indicated by the reports of examination, although workpaper evidence supporting the examination procedures performed was somewhat limited. OCC used its authority under PCA in an appropriate and timely manner but those actions ultimately did not save the bank.

All things considered, we believe that NBC acted in good faith when it invested in the government-sponsored-enterprise securities. Additionally, we have no reason to fault OCC's supervision of the institution as it relates to the bank's investment practices. Current law and regulatory standards permit banks to purchase government-sponsored-enterprise securities without limitation. What happened to Fannie Mae and Freddie Mac during the economic crisis, including the rapid decline in the value of their securities, was unprecedented. We reported that retrospectively, the lesson to be taken from the NBC material loss is that banks and regulators must be cognizant that securities not backed by the full faith and credit of the U.S. government entail risk and that high concentrations of such holdings elevate that risk.

We recommended that OCC (1) conduct a review of investments held by national banks for any potential high-risk concentrations and take appropriate supervisory action to mitigate the risk and (2) reassess examination guidance regarding investment securities, including government-sponsored-enterprise securities. OCC has taken steps to address our recommendations and plans to (1) reassess examination guidance regarding investment securities, including government-sponsored-enterprise securities, and (2) issue a supervisory memorandum containing supplemental examiner guidance on investment securities risk management practices. **(OIG-09-042)**

Recovery Act Audits

During the semiannual period, we completed one audit described below and initiated a number of other audits as part of our oversight of an estimated $22 billion in Treasury's non-

IRS spending authority under the American Recovery and Reinvestment Act of 2009. In addition to our mandated work, we consider our Recovery Act oversight a high-priority.

Treasury Has Made Progress in Implementing a Specified Energy Property Grant Program

Section 1603 of the Recovery Act provides for grants, in lieu of tax credits, to encourage taxpayers' continued investment in renewable energy sources and provides for reimbursement of a portion of the expenses incurred for placing eligible property in service. Treasury initially estimated that approximately $1 billion would be reimbursed under this new program. The program is administered by Treasury's Office of the Fiscal Assistant Secretary (OFAS).

Although the American Recovery and Reinvestment Act was intended to jumpstart the economy, we found—more than 5 months after the act was signed into law—that while Treasury had made progress, a fully operational program had yet to be established to meet the Recovery Act and OMB requirements. Among our concerns was OFAS's delay in finalizing an agreement with the Department of Energy to provide certain services in connection with the review of applications for reimbursement. OFAS also did not perform a proper risk assessment as required by OMB guidance or explain its current staffing level to implement and operate the program.

To address these matters, we recommended that OFAS (1) follow OMB guidance for identifying and prioritizing potential risks to the new program; (2) finalize its agreement with the Department of Energy and ensure that eligibility requirements are consistent with IRS requirements for tax credits; and (3) identify and address workforce needs to properly implement

the specified energy program and implement a
process to continuously evaluate those needs
throughout the program's life. OFAS
management concurred with two
recommendations and partially concurred with
the third. With respect to the partially concurred
recommendation, OFAS agreed that it was
important to identify and address workforce
needs and stated that it would continue to
evaluate its workforce. However, it also stated
that the current team of four was adequate.
(OIG-09-040)

Subsequent to our report, Treasury revised the
estimate of potential reimbursements under the
program to $16.5 billion.

Other Performance Audits

During this semiannual period, we completed a
joint audit with two other Intelligence
Community OIGs of a classified program and
issued a classified report. The audit was initiated
at the request of the Congress. Described below
are other performance audits completed during
the period.

OTS Involvement With Backdated Capital Contributions by Thrifts

We reviewed the circumstances surrounding the
backdating of capital contributions to prior
periods at six thrifts and concluded that the
backdating of these transactions was
inappropriate for all six thrifts.

For one thrift, BankUnited, FSB, the OTS
senior deputy director directed the regional
office to instruct the holding company to
contribute capital and backdate the transaction.
For another thrift, IndyMac Bank, FSB, an OTS
regional director authorized the backdating of
the transaction. For a third thrift, OTS objected

to backdating the transaction and informed the
thrift management not to do so, but the thrift
backdated it anyway. In this case and in two
other cases in which OTS became aware of the
backdating after the fact, OTS allowed the
backdating to remain. In one of these two other
cases, OTS did not become aware of the
backdating until after the period for amending
the thrift's financial reporting had closed. For
the sixth thrift that backdated a transaction,
OTS directed the thrift to reverse the
transaction when it became aware of the
backdating. In January 2009, OTS issued
guidance on the proper recognition of capital
contributions. OTS management was also
responsive to our other recommendations.
(OIG-09-037)

BankUnited, FSB, failed on May 21, 2009, after
our report was issued. The estimated loss to the
deposit insurance fund at the time of failure was
$4.9 billion. We are performing an MLR of
BankUnited, which was in progress at the end
of this semiannual reporting period.

City National Corporation Capital Purchase Program Case Study

As part of our interim oversight of TARP done
at the request of Secretary Paulson until the
office of the special inspector general for TARP
was in place, we initiated an audit of the
selection of the City National Corporation (City
National), the one-bank holding company for
City National Bank located in Los Angeles,
California, for participation in CPP. The
purpose of our work was to (1) provide a case
study of the approval process used by the
Office of Financial Stability for allowing City
National's participation in CPP and
(2) determine the controls in place to ensure
that the approval of this financial institution was

consistent with TARP objectives. City National received CPP funding of $400 million.

Based on our review, City National met the required criteria to receive CPP funding. At the time of the corporation's approval, limited policies and procedures were in place relating to the review and approval of TARP applications. We determined that OCC and the Office of Financial Stability followed those limited policies and procedures for approving City National for CPP. The Office of Financial Stability concurred with our findings and stated that additional controls for processing CPP applications had been implemented after City National was approved to receive funding. **(OIG-09-044)**

Community Development Financial Institutions Fund Contract Administration and Personnel Management Practices Need Improvement

We performed an audit of the Community Development Financial Institutions Fund to determine whether the Fund's contract administration practices for its information technology development and support contracts with General Dynamics and Kearney & Company complied with applicable regulations. Our audit was requested by the Fund Director.

The Fund could not provide documentary evidence supporting the contract administration activities performed by Fund contracting officer technical representatives for the General Dynamics contracts. As a result, the Fund could not demonstrate that the $19 million in contract dollars for information technology support services by the contractor were spent responsibly during the 9 year period from 1999 to 2008. Additionally, the Fund could not provide documentation showing how it determined that using three different federal

agencies since 1999 to perform the contracting officer functions for these contracts were in the best interest of the government. With respect to the $3.7 million Kearney & Company contract, we concluded that the Fund followed requirements.

Fund management concurred with our recommendations to address these contract administration deficiencies and planned to complete corrective actions by March 2010.

As another issue that surfaced during our review, we found that the Fund did not document its justification for a noncompetitive promotion of a Fund employee to GS-14 in July 2006 and was unable to provide us with the employee's related position description during our review. Fund management agreed to implement controls to prevent a reoccurrence and ensure valid position descriptions are on file for all employees. **(OIG-09-048)**

The Mint Subleased Excessive Space in Its Headquarters Building (Corrective Action Verification on OIG-02-074)

In March 2002, we reported that the Mint had leased excessive space for its headquarters operations and recommended, among other things, that the Mint sublease the excessive space. In a follow-up review, we found that the Mint had consolidated its headquarters operations, sublet more space to federal agencies, and, during our review, awarded a sublease for the remaining excess space. We also reported that particular space had remained vacant for 12 years, representing a loss of approximately $5 million in potential rent revenue during the period. **(OIG-09-046)**

Significant Investigations

Guilty Plea Entered by Derrick Hampton

On June 12, 2009, Derrick Hampton, who was formerly employed as a secretary by OCC, pled guilty to federal theft violations stemming from his scheme to defraud OCC by exploiting a weakness he found in its travel management system. Immediately following the plea, Hampton was sentenced to 60 days of house arrest, 36 months of supervised probation, 25 hours of community service and was ordered to pay $25,311 in restitution to OCC. This successful court action concludes the investigation that we initiated after an OCC internal review indicated that Hampton may have been reimbursed for travel expenses that had never been incurred. Our investigation identified 19 fraudulent travel claims, totaling $25,311 that OCC paid to the employee. As a result of the investigation and internal review, OCC implemented internal controls intended to better identify potential fraudulent claims and prevent future exploitation of vulnerabilities.

Subject Indicted After Exploiting FMS Systems

On July 9, 2009, Michael Lunsford was indicted in Marion County, Indiana, for 10 state violations related to financial fraud and theft. The charges followed our investigation that revealed that Lunsford used a compromised routing transit number belonging to FMS to purchase several new cars from a local auto dealership. We initiated the investigation after the Treasury Inspector General for Tax Administration referred information to us that a Treasury state tax offset program routing transit number had been compromised by numerous individuals, including Lunsford. As a result of the events that led to our investigation, FMS independently instituted a series of more stringent internal controls to prevent similar compromises in the future.

U.S. Mint Employee Charged With Federal Fraud and Theft Violations

On July 23, 2009, a Mint supply specialist was arraigned in the U.S. District Court for the Eastern District of Pennsylvania after being charged with federal violations related to his conflicts of interest, false statements, honest services fraud, wire fraud, and mail fraud. The employee pled not guilty to the charges and was released on a $20,000 bond. The supply specialist was charged after our investigation revealed that the employee structured office supply orders to total approximately $4,999 (one dollar less than the single-purchase limit) to deliberately circumvent the competitive bidding process and direct purchases to a company owned by a former Mint employee.

The following are updates of significant investigative activities that occurred in prior semiannual reporting periods.

Court Actions Progress in Postal Theft Conspiracy Targeting Treasury Checks

As previously reported, 13 subjects were indicted on June 19, 2008, for federal mail fraud, identity theft, aiding and abetting, and forgery violations stemming from the subject's theft and conversion of Treasury checks. The indictment resulted from a joint investigation conducted by our office, the U.S. Secret Service, and the U.S. Postal Inspection Service, which revealed an extensive conspiracy to steal Treasury checks from the U.S. mail and convert them to cash through the use of stolen identities. To date, 11 defendants have pled guilty to their participation in this scheme and 6 have been sentenced.

Updates

- On March 2, 2009, Chamarko Amin was arrested in Washington, DC. Amin had been a fugitive since his 2008 indictment. On August 7, 2009, Amin pled guilty to conspiracy to commit mail fraud and aggravated identity theft in connection with the scheme and is scheduled to be sentenced on October 23, 2009.

- On July 22, 2009, Leonard Jenkins pled guilty to mail fraud, theft of mail, and aggravated identity theft in connection with his participation in a scheme in which he used his position as a mail carrier to steal over $100,000 of Treasury checks from the U.S. mail. Jenkins faces a maximum sentence of 20 years in prison for conspiracy to commit mail fraud, 5 years in prison for theft of mail by a postal employee, and a mandatory 2 years in prison consecutive to any other sentence imposed for aggravated identity theft. Sentencing is scheduled for November 3, 2009.

- On August 6, 2009, Tandria Boyd was convicted by a jury on charges related to conspiracy to commit mail fraud, mail fraud, forged endorsement on a Treasury check, and aggravated identity theft for her role in the scheme. Boyd's sentencing is pending.

- On August 7, 2009, Michael Hawkins was sentenced to 4 years of federal incarceration followed by 3 years of supervised release for conspiracy to commit mail fraud, forged endorsement on a Treasury check, and aggravated identity theft in connection with the scheme.

Sentencing for Bank Fraud and Identity Theft

As previously reported, our office and the U.S. Secret Service conducted a joint investigation that revealed that Osman Jalloh used false identification documents to fraudulently open numerous accounts at Bank of America and Chevy Chase Bank. Subsequently, Jalloh used those accounts to successfully negotiate 10 Treasury checks, along with numerous personal checks, that had been stolen from the New Jersey area. The joint investigation identified 22 victims, with total attempted fraud losses of $295,453, and resulted in Jalloh's August 25, 2008, indictment in the District of Maryland for his participation in the stolen check scheme.

Update

On May 1, 2009, Jalloh pled guilty to one count of bank fraud. Following his plea, on July 20, 2009, Jalloh was sentenced to 48 months of federal incarceration followed by 5 years of supervised release.

Other OIG Accomplishments and Activity

Inspector General Thorson Testifies on the Material Loss Review Threshold

On May 5, 2009, Inspector General Thorson testified before the Subcommittee on Oversight and Investigations of the House Committee on Financial Services in a hearing titled *The Role of Inspectors General: Minimizing and Mitigating Waste, Fraud and Abuse*. The inspectors general for the FDIC and the Federal Reserve System also testified at the hearing. The subject of Mr. Thorson's testimony was the threshold for MLRs of failed banks. In January 2009, the three inspectors general sent a letter to the committee suggesting that the current threshold of $25 million, established in 1991, be raised to between $300 million and $500 million, which would free up resources for other work.

In his testimony, Mr. Thorson stressed the importance of MLRs and described the impact of the unprecedented number of MLRs during the current crisis to our office's ability to do other work. For example, work deferred includes all work on Treasury's anti-money laundering and terrorist financing mission. Mr. Thorson also expressed support for increasing the MLR threshold.

Congress is considering legislation, H.R. 3330, that would, among other things, raise the threshold loss for MLRs to $200 million. As of September 30, 2009, H.R. 3330 had passed the House and has been referred to the Senate Committee on Banking, Housing, and Urban Affairs.

OIG Conducts Inquiries at Request of Senator Grassley

During this reporting period, the OIG completed two inquires at the request of Senator Charles Grassley, Ranking Minority Member of the Senate Finance Committee. The first concerned the issuance, in October 2008, of IRS Notice 2008-83, which provided guidance on the application of Internal Revenue Code Section 382(h) regarding the recognition of losses incurred by failed banks that were acquired by other banks. This guidance engendered much critical comment in the industry and in Congress, and was ultimately nullified in the American Recovery and Reinvestment Act. The OIG inquiry set out the process by which the guidance was developed and promulgated by the IRS and the Department's Office of Tax Policy.

The second inquiry focused on the role of the Department's Office of General Counsel in reviewing the legal underpinnings of the retention bonuses paid to certain employees of the Financial Products subsidiary of AIG, a company which had received billions of dollars in federal assistance after incurring large losses. This event had also engendered much critical comment. The OIG inquiry determined that the Office of General Counsel reviewed and concurred with the opinion of a private law firm which concluded that applicable state law compelled the payment of the bonuses.

OIG Hosts Delegation From Vietnam

In April 2009, Inspector General Eric Thorson and OIG executives met with a delegation from Vietnam to discuss the mission of U.S. government inspectors general and Treasury OIG. Members of the delegation from the Government Inspectorate of Vietnam were Mr.

Lam Ngoc Bui, Acting Director General (Bureau II); Mr. Son Hung Dang, Division Head, Anti-Corruption Bureau; Mr. Toan Khanh Dang, Deputy Director General (Department II); Mr. Cong Trong Ha, Director General, Department for International Cooperation; Dr. Minh Van Tran, Deputy Director General (Bureau III); Mr. Truyen Van Tran, General; and Ms. Hoa Nhu Trinh, Division Head, Department for International Cooperation. Also in the delegation were Mr. Trac Ngoc Kieu, Vice Chairman, Steering Committee on Prevention and Combat Against Corruption; Mr. Truong Xuan Lam, Chief Inspector of Ho Chi Minh City; and Mr. Ngoc Hong Nguyen, Vice Chairman, Subcommittee on Inspection, Party Committee of Ho Chi Minh City. Treasury's Departmental Offices International Visitors Program facilitated the meeting.

Meeting With Representative From Bhutan Commission

In May 2009, Deputy Inspector General Dennis Schindel and Counsel Rich Delmar met with Ms. Neten Zangmo, chair of the Bhutan Anti-Corruption Commission, to provide information on investigating allegations of corruption and other misconduct.

OIG Executives Participate in Professional Audit Organizations

The Federal Audit Executive Council (FAEC) consists of audit executives from the OIG community and other federal audit organizations. Its purpose is to discuss and coordinate issues affecting the federal audit community, with special emphasis on audit policy and operations of common interest to FAEC members. During the period, Treasury OIG continued to actively support a number of

FAEC initiatives. Marla Freedman, Assistant Inspector General for Audit, serves on the executive board, which coordinates the activities of FAEC's working committees. Joel Grover, Deputy Assistant Inspector General for Financial Management and Information Technology Audits, serves as co-chair of the FAEC Financial Statements Committee and is actively involved in developing and coordinating FAEC positions on a variety of accounting and auditing issues related to federal financial reporting.

Mr. Grover is also a member of the Government Performance and Accountability Committee of the American Institute of Certified Public Accountants (AICPA). The committee's mission is to (1) promote greater government accountability and integrity of government operations, information, and information systems; (2) promote and encourage increased participation and involvement by certified public accountants (CPA) in government within AICPA; (3) enhance the professional image and value of CPAs in government; (4) provide advice and counsel to AICPA on the needs of CPAs in government, and (5) serve as a conduit for communications among CPAs in government, AICPA, and other professional organizations. Mr. Grover is also co-chair of the Maryland Association of Certified Public Accountants Members in Government Committee. The committee's activities include sponsoring an annual training conference on government/not-for-profit accounting and auditing issues.

Statistical Summary

Summary of OIG Activity

For the 6 months ended September 30, 2009

OIG Activity	Number or Dollar Value
Office of Counsel Activity	
Regulation and legislation reviews	1
Instances where information was refused	0
Office of Audit Activities	
Reports issued (audits and evaluations)	19
Disputed audit recommendations	0
Significant revised management decisions	0
Management decision in which the IG disagrees	0
Monetary benefits (audit)	
Questioned costs	$995,367
Funds put to better use	0
Revenue enhancements	0
Total monetary benefits	$995,367
Office of Investigations Activities	
Allegations	
Total allegations received and processed	135
Cases—investigations and inquiries (including joint investigations)	
Opened in the reporting period	27
Closed in the reporting period	32
Total cases in progress as of 9/30/2009	164
Criminal and judicial actions (including joint investigations)	
Cases referred for prosecution and/or litigation	16
Cases accepted for prosecution and/or litigation	0
Arrests	2
Indictments/informations	3
Convictions (by trial and plea)	16
Fines/restitution/recoveries (including joint investigations)	$234,504
Administrative sanctions	
Total adverse personnel actions taken	27
Oversight activities	
Prevention and detection briefings	2
Quality assessment reviews	0
Management implication reports	0

Significant Unimplemented Recommendations

For reports issued prior to October 1, 2008

The following list of OIG audit reports with unimplemented recommendations is based on information in Treasury's automated audit recommendation tracking system, which is maintained by Treasury management officials.

Number	Date	Report Title and Recommendation Summary
OIG-06-030	05/06	*Terrorist Financing/Money Laundering: FinCEN Has Taken Steps to Better Analyze Bank Secrecy Act Data but Challenges Remain* FinCEN should enhance the current FinCEN database system or acquire a new system. An improved system should provide for complete and accurate information on the case type, status, resources, and time expended in performing the analysis. This system should also have the proper security controls to maintain integrity of the data. (1 recommendation)
OIG-07-048	9/07	*Foreign Assets Control: Actions Have Been Taken to Better Ensure Financial Institution Compliance With OFAC Sanction Programs, But Their Effectiveness Cannot Yet Be Determined* The OFAC Director should determine whether MOUs should be established with self-regulatory organizations and IRS for sharing information on financial institutions for which they have OFAC oversight responsibility. (1 recommendation)
OIG-08-008	11/07	*Management Letter for Fiscal Year 2007 Audit of the Federal Financing Bank's Financial Statements* The Federal Financing Bank should do the following: (1) Continue its efforts in developing a system development methodology and a configuration management plan. The system development methodology should describe programming naming conventions, the system development phases and what is to be performed in each, procedures for handling emergency programming changes, application test procedures, and development, test and production of access controls lists, etc., as documented in NIST SP 800-64. (2) Follow through with its plan to upgrade the LMCS Database Management System to a supported version of Oracle. (3) Configure LMCS to require users to use at least eight-character passwords and implement all of the required configurations of Treasury Directive Publication 85-01, including complex passwords and user session

timeouts, or perform an evaluation to determine the risk of not having all of the required configurations implemented. (3 recommendations)

OIG-08-018   12/07   *Management Letter for the Fiscal Year 2007 Audit of the United States Mint's Financial Statements*
Mint management should establish and implement policies and procedures for the retirement of assets to ensure that Excess Property forms are properly completed, filed, and available for examination for a reasonable time period after the retirement transaction. (1 recommendation)

OIG-08-031   04/08   *Review of Treasury's Failure to Provide Congress Required Quadrennial Reports in 1998 and 2002 on Foreign Acquisitions and Industrial Espionage Activity Involving U.S. Critical Technology Companies*
Treasury should ensure that internal Committee on Foreign Investments in the United States guidance for implementing the Foreign Investment and National Security Act of 2007 is established and includes procedures for preparing and issuing the annual report to Congress on foreign investment in critical technology companies and industrial espionage activities. (1 recommendation)

OIG-08-036   06/08   *BEP Needs to Enforce and Strengthen Controls on Its Eastern Currency Facility to Prevent and Detect Employee Theft*
BEP should direct BEP management to (1) establish clear, written policies and procedures that specify assignment of responsibility and actions to be taken when discrepancies are found in the production process and (2) ensure that employees, including supervisors, are trained and periodically retrained in product security-related policies and procedures. (2 recommendations)

OIG-08-046   09/08   *Federal Information Security Management Act Fiscal Year 2008 Performance Audit*
OIG recommended that (1) OTS continue with bureau plans to resolve the security weaknesses identified during the certification and accreditation process by the end of the interim authorization period, December 31, 2008, and achieve a full authority to operate during the fiscal year 2009 FISMA reporting period, and (2) Departmental Offices, FinCEN, OIG, and OTS work to implement Federal Desktop Core Configurations secure

configuration baselines on all Microsoft Windows XP workstations.
(2 recommendations)

OIG-CA-08-012 09/08   *FY 2008 Evaluation of Treasury's FISMA Implementation for Its Non-IRS Non-Intelligence National Security Systems*
The Treasury Chief Information Officer should ensure implementation of Federal Desktop Core Configuration security settings on all applicable non-intelligence National Security Systems in accordance with bureau-established plans. (1 recommendation)

Summary of Instances Where Information Was Refused

April 1, 2009, through September 30, 2009

There were no such instances during this period.

Listing of Audit and Evaluation Reports Issued

April 1, 2009, through September 30, 2009

Financial Audits and Reports on the Processing of Transactions by BPD

Controls Placed in Operation and Tests of Operating Effectiveness for the Bureau of the Public Debt's Administrative Resource Center for the Period July 1, 2008, to June 30, 2009, OIG-09-045, 8/28/09

Report on Controls Placed in Operation and Tests of Operating Effectiveness for the Bureau of the Public Debt's Trust Funds Management Branch for the Period August 1, 2008, to July 31, 2009, OIG-09-049, 9/23/09

Report on Controls Placed in Operation and Tests of Operating Effectiveness for the Bureau of the Public Debt's Federal Investments Branch for the Period August 1, 2008, to July 31, 2009, OIG-09-050, 9/23/09

Information Technology Audits and Evaluations

Fiscal Year 2009 Evaluation of Treasury's FISMA Implementation for Its Intelligence Program, OIG-CA-09-011, 7/17/09

FMS's Database Management Systems Have Weaknesses in Key Controls, OIG-CA-09-012, 9/29/09

Fiscal Year 2009 Audit of Treasury's FISMA Implementation for Its Non-IRS Collateral National Security Systems, OIG-09-051, 9/30/09

Performance Audits

Safety and Soundness: Material Loss Review of Ameribank, Inc., OIG-09-036, 4/7/09

Safety and Soundness: OTS Involvement With Backdated Capital Contributions by Thrifts, OIG-09-037, 5/21/09

Safety and Soundness: Material Loss Review of PFF Bank and Trust, OIG-09-038, 6/12/09

Safety and Soundness: Material Loss Review of Downey Savings and Loan, FA, OIG-09-039, 6/15/09

Joint Review of a Classified Program, 6/30/09

Treasury Has Made Progress in Implementing the Specified Energy Property Grant Program, OIG-09-040, 8/5/09

Safety and Soundness: Material Loss Review of National Bank of Commerce, OIG-09-042, 8/6/09

Safety and Soundness: Material Loss Review of Ocala National Bank, OIG-09-043, 8/26/09

Safety and Soundness: City National Corporation Capital Purchase Program Case Study, OIG-09-044, 8/27/09

General Management: The Mint Subleased Excessive Space in Its Headquarters Building (Corrective Action Verification on OIG-02-074), OIG-09-046, 9/3/09

Safety and Soundness: Material Loss Review of Suburban Federal Savings Bank, OIG-09-047, 9/11/09

CDFI Fund Contract Administration and Personnel Management Practices Need Improvement, OIG-09-048, 9/17/09

Supervised Contract Audit

Contract Audit: Spectra Systems Corporation's Cost Proposal in Response to Solicitation TEP-09-007, OIG-09-040A, 7/15/09, **$995,367 Q**

Audit Reports Issued With Questioned Costs

April 1, 2009, through September 30, 2009

Category	Total No. of Reports	Total Questioned Costs[a]	Total Unsupported Costs[a]
For which no management decision had been made by beginning of reporting period	2	$461,973	0
Which were issued during the reporting period[b]	1	$995,367	0
Subtotals	3	$1,457,340	0
For which a management decision was made during the reporting period	2	$461,973	0
Dollar value of disallowed costs	2	$461,973	0
Dollar value of costs not disallowed	0	0	0
For which no management decision was made by the end of the reporting period	1	$995,367	0
For which no management decision was made within 6 months of issuance	0	0	0

[a] Questioned costs include unsupported costs.

[b] Audit was performed by the Defense Contract Audit Agency.

Audit Reports Issued With Recommendations That Funds Be Put to Better Use

April 1, 2009, through September 30, 2009

At the beginning of the period, there were no audit reports from prior periods pending a management decision on recommendations that funds be put to better use. There were also no audit reports issued during this period with recommendations that funds be put to better use.

Previously Issued Audit Reports Pending Management Decisions (Over 6 Months)

As of September 30, 2009

There were no audit reports issued before this semiannual reporting period that are pending a management decision.

Significant Revised Management Decisions

April 1, 2009, through September 30, 2009

There were no significant revised management decisions during the period.

Significant Disagreed Management Decisions

April 1, 2009, through September 30, 2009

There were no management decisions this period with which the IG was in disagreement.

References to the Inspector General Act

	Requirement	Page
Section 4(a)(2)	Review of legislation and regulations	22
Section 5(a)(1)	Significant problems, abuses, and deficiencies	6-19
Section 5(a)(2)	Recommendations with respect to significant problems, abuses, and deficiencies	6-19
Section 5(a)(3)	Significant unimplemented recommendations described in previous semiannual reports	23-25
Section 5(a)(4)	Matters referred to prosecutive authorities	22
Section 5(a)(5)	Summary of instances where information was refused	25
Section 5(a)(6)	List of audit reports	25-26
Section 5(a)(7)	Summary of significant reports	6-19
Section 5(a)(8)	Audit reports with questioned costs	27
Section 5(a)(9)	Recommendations that funds be put to better use	27
Section 5(a)(10)	Summary of audit reports issued before the beginning of the reporting period for which no management decision had been made	27
Section 5(a)(11)	Significant revised management decisions made during the reporting period	28
Section 5(a)(12)	Management decisions with which the IG is in disagreement	28
Section 5(a)(13)	Instances of unresolved FFMIA noncompliance	7
Section 5(d)	Serious or flagrant problems, abuses, or deficiencies	N/A
Section 6(b)(2)	Report to Secretary when information or assistance is unreasonably refused	N/A

Abbreviations

AICPA	American Institute of Certified Public Accountants
BPD	Bureau of the Public Debt
BSA	Bank Secrecy Act
CPA	certified public accountant
CPP	Capital Purchase Program
EESA	Emergency Economic Stabilization Act
FAEC	Federal Audit Executive Council
FDIC	Federal Deposit Insurance Corporation
FDICIA	Federal Deposit Insurance Corporation Improvement Act
FinCEN	Financial Crimes Enforcement Network
FISMA	Federal Information Security Management Act
FMS	Financial Management Service
GAO	Government Accountability Office
IPA	independent public accountant
IRS	Internal Revenue Service
MLR	Material Loss Review
OCC	Office of the Comptroller of the Currency
OFAC	Office of Foreign Assets Control
OFAS	Office of the Fiscal Assistant Secretary
OIG	Office of Inspector General
OMB	Office of Management and Budget
OTS	Office of Thrift Supervision
PCA	Prompt Corrective Action
TARP	Troubled Assets Relief Program

View of Alexander Hamilton statue from south side of main Treasury building

contact us

Headquarters
Office of Inspector General
1500 Pennsylvania Avenue, N.W.,
Room 4436
Washington, D.C. 20220
Phone: (202) 622-1090;
Fax: (202) 622-2151

Office of Audit
740 15th Street, N.W., Suite 600
Washington, D.C. 20220
Phone: (202) 927-5400;
Fax: (202) 927-5379

Office of Investigations
740 15th Street, N.W., Suite 500
Washington, D.C. 20220
Phone: (202) 927-5260;
Fax: (202) 927-5421

Office of Counsel
740 15th Street, N.W., Suite 510
Washington, D.C. 20220
Phone: (202) 927-0650;
Fax: (202) 927-5418

Office of Management
740 15th Street, N.W., Suite 510
Washington, D.C. 20220

Phone: (202) 927-5200;
Fax: (202) 927-6492

Eastern Field Audit Office
408 Atlantic Avenue, Room 330
Boston, Massachusetts 02110-3350
Phone: (617) 223-8640;
Fax (617) 223-8651

Treasury OIG Hotline
Call Toll Free: 1.800.359.3898

Treasury OIG Web Page

OIG reports and other information are now available via the
Internet. The address is
http://www.treas.gov/inspector-general

www.ingramcontent.com/pod-product-compliance
Lightning Source LLC
Chambersburg PA
CBHW052022280526
45793CB00005B/1087